TAI CHI

PAUL CROMPTON

PETER ALBRIGHT, M.D., SERIES EDITOR

MACMILLAN • USA

A QUARTO BOOK

Copyright © 1996 by Quarto Inc.

MACMILLAN
A Simon and Schuster Macmillan Company
1633 Broadway
New York, NY 10019-6785

ISBN 0-02-860831-3

The book was designed and produced by
Quarto Inc.
The Old Brewery
6 Blundell Street
London N7 9BH

Senior Editor Sally MacEachern
Editor Alison Leach
Editorial Assistant Judith Evans
Indexer Dorothy Frame
Senior art editor Penny Cobb
Designer Alyson Kyles
Picture researcher Susannah Jayes
Illustrators Sally Launder, Sharon Smith, Samantha Elmhurst
Photographers Paul Forrester, Peter Barry, Laura Wickenden
Models Rhonda Bailey, Paul Crompton
Picture research manager Giulia Hetherington
Editorial director Mark Dartford
Art director Moira Clinch

Typeset by Central Southern Typesetters, Eastbourne
Manufactured in Hong Kong by Regent Publishing Services Ltd
Printed in China by Leefung-Asco Printers Ltd

10 9 8 7 6 5 4 3 2 1

CONTENTS

INTRODUCTION

For many thousands of people, all over the world, the yin-yang symbol represents the ancient Chinese art of Tai Chi Chuan. The words mean "Supreme Ultimate Fist." "Chuan" (fist) means much more than a clenched hand. To a Chinese person, it means "studies and training associated with a martial art." However, Tai Chi, as it is generally called, is frequently used for improving and maintaining health; and it is in this aspect that it is presented in this book. It *can* be used for fighting.

Tai Chi Chuan in Chinese calligraphy.

Like a great deal of Chinese culture, Tai Chi is surrounded with legend. This often obscures its history. Legend sees Tai Chi originating in the dreams of the Taoist Immortal, Chang San-Feng, some 800 years ago. Scholarly theory proposes a number of earlier dates and causes. But more recent historical research places the beginnings of the art at the end of the eighteenth century or the early part of the nineteenth.

FOUNDER FAMILIES

In China, styles of martial arts frequently "belonged" to a particular family. The methods and techniques produced by a particular family were guarded from all outsiders. It is the Chen family who are regarded as the founders of Tai Chi. In those early days, the art was simply a powerful, combative mode of exercise and fighting. Later in the nineteenth century, a member of the Yang family was admitted to the Chen Tai Chi circle. Thus, the Yang family became heirs, guardians, and students, producing their own versions of Tai Chi.

Like all Chinese martial arts, Tai Chi has aspects devoted to the use of weapons, the most popular of these being the straight, double-edged sword. Swordsmanship is highly regarded in China. A sword has almost magical qualities and should be used with respect. There is also another sword, curved like a scimitar, a long pole or staff, a spear, and a halberd.

Slowly, Tai Chi developed a purely health and exercise aspect. More "outsiders" gained entry, and other styles appeared, notably Wu, Sun, and Hao. Today, these five – Chen, Yang, Wu, Sun, and Hao – are the best known. Of these, the Yang style is the most widely taught.

Among Western people, the most familiar version of the Yang style is that created by Chen Man-ch'ing, a Chinese artist, physician, and scholar who spent much time in the United States. However, during the 1950s, leading Chinese Tai Chi experts met and produced a number of Tai Chi Forms or movement sequences. These were graded in terms of degree of difficulty and length. Since then, these Forms have been gaining in popularity. The Form presented in this book is the 24-Step Beijing, or Simplified, Tai Chi Form, the first of this modern series.

From early in the morning, Chinese people do Tai Chi in parks.

UNDERSTANDING THE FORM

A Form consists of a number of postures which are connected together so that a continuous chain of movement takes place. It can be compared to a map, in which the roads are the connecting movements and the postures are the towns passed through. Each posture has a name, such as "White Crane Spreads Its Wings." The way in which one moves is the key to everything.

This helps to explain the difference between Tai Chi as a fighting art, Tai Chi as a health exercise, and Tai Chi as a means of spiritual development. If someone were to try to hit you on the head with a club, you could lift your arms very fast and block the attack. This might prevent your receiving a head injury, but in making this movement, you might strain your muscles. If you made the same movement, alone and undisturbed, moving very slowly, relaxed and paying attention – moving in fact in the best possible way for your joints and muscles – the result for your body would be quite different. And, again, if you were to make an identical movement

which was associated with a Taoist meditation exercise, then another result would follow.

One can say that the first of these movements represents the Chen family style, which was aimed at fighting and the development of fluid power. The

Combining the spiritual aspects of Tai Chi with the physical movements of the Form gives powerful results.

Yang family style contains this element, but it also contains the second and third elements of health and spiritual development. If you study Tai Chi, the teacher's own preferences will inevitably prevail. The 24-Step Beijing Form is aimed at finding health and relaxation.

THE FORM

A continuous chain of movements makes up a Form.

PUSH HANDS

Less well-known in the Tai Chi syllabus is Push Hands. This is a method of training with a partner. In Push Hands you rest one or two palms on the wrist and forearm of your partner and push him or her backward. In the beginning, this is done with very little force. Your partner must stay in contact with your palms, and give way or yield to your push. When your partner has shifted back as far as is comfortably possible, he or she then pushes you and in turn you yield. In time, more complex combinations of movements are added to this simple one.

The basis of such training lies in the early combative aspects of Tai Chi, but in my view it also has psychological implications connected with how people interact with each other. These are outside the scope of this book. All the movements are done according to certain basic principles (pages 8–11).

In the Tai Chi "world," there are competitions where students present a Form and are awarded points for excellence. This is comparable to ice-skating or track and field events seen on television. The judges look for the basic elements and principles of Tai Chi movement, and any departure from these factors, in making their decisions.

Push Hands teaches you how to relax under pressure.

BASIC PRINCIPLES

When an animal moves one part of its body – for instance, its head – the whole body follows this movement or adjusts to it. Civilized people for the most part do not achieve this: their movements are usually disjointed and exaggerated. This is because people have lost contact with their innate capacity to move naturally. It is as though each set of muscles has a mind of its own, controlled by humans' emotional states, sudden thoughts, and reactions built up over decades of misuse.

In Tai Chi, efforts are made to correct this and to return to the softness and pliability of childhood. A major element of this is to learn how to move the whole body as one unit. When you turn your body in the Tai Chi Form, the whole body turns. This produces smoothness and harmony; and this materially affects the flow of blood, energy, and breathing. Instead of each muscle group having a "mind of its own," there is one "mind" or one thought permeating the movement, and this thought is one of unity of action.

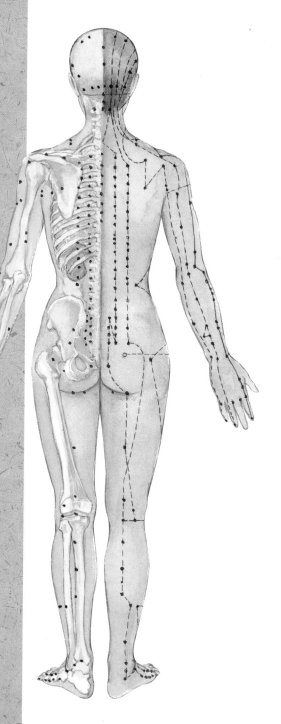

Chi flows along the meridians through the many specialized points.

THE CHI FLOW

A fundamental concept of Traditional Chinese Medicine is *Chi*. This is translated as "intrinsic energy." It is an energy that is not recognized by modern Western medical thinking, but is, for instance, basic to Chinese acupuncture treatment. In Traditional Chinese Medicine, the human body is covered and penetrated by channels (*Chinglo*). These invisible channels conduct the *Chi* energy to all parts of the body. *Chi* assists the various organs and fluids of the body to function correctly.

When one of the channels is blocked, the *Chi* cannot flow. When a channel is opened too much, there is too much *Chi*. When an area is inactive through a blockage, then there will be a buildup of stagnant *Chi*. The subject of *Chi* is a vast one, and only an oversimplified picture can be given in a book of this length.

However, this explanation will serve to illustrate the maxim that in Tai Chi, the *Chi* flows downward.

This means that among educated people there is an overabundance of energy and activity, and therefore *Chi*, in the upper part of the body and the brain. This activity is fiery and agitated.

The lower part of the body is seen as being calmer, like water. By assisting the *Chi* to flow downward, Tai Chi aims to bring the fire down into the lower part of the body and the water up into the torso and brain. This is echoed in the Zen saying, "Cool head, warm feet." Such a practice is also connected with the principle of "Rooting" (page 55).

The bones of the body should be correctly aligned. This alignment cannot be achieved overnight. It comes through training.

CORRECT ALIGNMENT

To assist the flow of *Chi* further, the bones of the body should be correctly aligned. The head "floats upward as if suspended from above by a single hair." The upper back is "lifted." The lower back is vertical, the abdomen rounded, and the knees slightly bent, taking the tension out of them.

This alignment cannot be achieved overnight. It comes through training. In Tai Chi, the body and psyche receive new messages; and as these messages get through, the whole being tends to move in the direction of the basic principles. It is a method of re-education and can only happen slowly, since there are years of moving wrong to contend with.

YIN AND YANG

Probably the oldest Chinese philosophical theory is that of Yin and Yang, yin being feminine, shaded, passive, and soft; and yang being masculine, sunlit, active, and hard. This concept divides all phenomena into yin and yang. It is a very useful classification. For instance, if a muscle is contracted to its maximum, it is in an extreme yang condition. Fully relaxed and passive, it will be in an extreme yin condition.

As soon as the muscle begins to contract or relax, it starts to lose some of its yin or yang qualities and acquire those of its opposite. In shifting the weight from one leg to another while performing the Tai Chi Forms, the legs move from one condition to another as the weight is transferred. The arms, back, abdomen, and joints experience similar changes.

This alternation of yin and yang helps the *Chi* to flow naturally and reach all the organs, tissues, and fluids of the body, without forcing. Similarly, as the lungs empty and fill, they exemplify the same principle.

Probably the oldest Chinese philosophical theory is that of Yin and Yang.

I-Ching

Looking around you, as the Chinese philosophers did, you can see the same phenomenon in Nature with the round of seasons, waxing and waning of the moon, rising and setting of the sun, ebb and flow of the tides, and so forth. It is not difficult to see that through Tai Chi, human beings can take part in something fundamental in the universe: the Supreme Ultimate. This idea can be found in the most famous Chinese book, the *I-Ching*, or Book of Changes. Revered by Confucius and consulted by millions of people, the *I-Ching* stems from eight simple diagrams (trigrams). These represent various combinations of yin and yang by means of lines. A single unbroken line is yang, and a single broken line is yin. The ultimate yang condition has three parallel unbroken lines and the yin three parallel broken lines.

Some teachers of Tai Chi relate the different movements of the Forms to the eight basic trigrams of the *I-Ching*. Thus the strongest movement would be a yang sign and the most yielding movement a yin sign. There is no uniform agreement about this, but it is nevertheless a part of Tai Chi thinking.

I-CHING (THE BOOK OF CHANGES)

earth   heaven

wind   thunder

fire   water

lake   mountain

The Mind Leads the Chi

In most sports the aim is for the movements to become spontaneous. This is partly because the actions are relatively quick. In Tai Chi the movements are usually slow, apart from those in the Chen style. This means that there is time for some form of mental activity. Left to itself, conditioned as it is, your body would perform Tai Chi movements in the same way as it usually performs other actions. In other words, none of the principles would be observed.

In learning the actions of Tai Chi, you should at the same time learn to watch or keep an eye on the quality of those actions. You should try to move with a minimum of tension, moving all the body at the same time and reproducing the postures accurately. If you notice that a particular movement creates a strong and unnecessary tension, work at releasing that tension and finding out how you are causing it.

The mind (yi) leads the chi as the movement is performed.

INTRODUCTORY EXERCISES

Perhaps the best way to begin Tai Chi is to look at your own naked body in front of a mirror. Move all the joints that you are aware of and see how they work. The following exercises do not cause strain and are specially designed to make use of almost all the joints and muscles in a similar way to the actions of Tai Chi.

Move the hands slowly as you scoop rice, sensing the grains on your skin.

1 Place your left heel down in front of you, keeping the sole raised. Keep the knee straight, not bent.

JOINTS

All the major joints of the body open and close. For instance, as the muscles contract, the upper and lower arms will get closer to one another or farther apart. When you bend your elbow, the elbow joint closes, and as you straighten the elbow, the joint opens.

This type of activity is seen as a "pump" for the *Chi* flow. Closing restricts and confines the *Chi,* and opening sends it along its natural direction. You will make many of these types of movements in the Form. The exercises on these pages, which are purely repetitive, will give you an introduction to this.

2 Bend your right knee, and at the same time lower the sole of your left foot to the floor. As you do so, relax your left leg as much as possible.

3 Shift your full weight onto your left leg, bending the knee. Raise the heel of your right foot. Repeat steps 1-3 on the other side.

POINTS

Continue to walk at a slow, even pace, following the contraction and relaxation of the legs. • Relax your chest, pectoral muscles, shoulders, and abdomen. Relax your facial muscles and gaze toward the horizon. • Do not fix your gaze; simply do not focus on anything visual. • This exercise requires no particular ability or strength; it simply requires your alert and continuous attention.

If you follow it for some minutes, you will find that your body has a tendency to relax much more deeply, and a feeling of peacefulness may develop. • Make absolutely sure that you are dividing the movements clearly from one another. At first, do not attempt to slide from one to the next.

OPENING AND CLOSING THE JOINTS

1 Let your arms hang down at your sides in a normal standing position. Relax and look into the middle distance.

2 Bend at the hips as shown. Let your arms hang and relax your chest muscles. Then straighten up.

POINTS

Move slowly and continuously.
• Do not hold your breath; breathe naturally. • Keep your whole back naturally straight, making no artificial "joints" in the spine. • Keep your neck and head in line with the spine. • Keep your knees over the arch of your foot, as shown left. • As you close the hip-groin joints, imagine you are gathering in energy. • As you open (stand up), imagine you are releasing energy.
• Do not force anything, and if you are not fit, make only a small bend; you do not get a prize if you go deeper than anyone else – only joint problems!

SCOOPING UP RICE

1 From a normal standing position, step forward with your left foot. Keep most of your weight on the right.

2 Curve your palms as if they were scoops for rice or flour and shift your weight onto the left leg.

3 Lean forward, slowly plunging your hands into an imaginary tub of rice, as in the illustration.

4 Lift the rice up and begin to shift your weight back onto your right foot. As you move backward, turn your palms over as if letting the rice drop back into the tub.

5 As you complete the weight shift, lift the left toes off the ground so that your left leg rests on the heel.

POINTS

Move at a slow, even speed.
• As you complete the weight shift forward, your rear leg, spine, and head should be in a relatively straight line – no artificial "joints" in the back. • When your hands scoop, lift, and drop the rice, your forearm rotates gradually at the elbow, like a corkscrew or drill.

1 Make a "beak" with both hands. Rise up onto the balls of your feet, lifting your arms up in front of you, above your head.

2 Spread your arms sideways, opening the palms to face downward.

3 Sink down with feet flat on the floor, arms descending.

4 Move up again onto the balls of your feet, raising your arms in front of you, with the palms up, as high as your waist.

5 Turn your palms over and press them backward behind your buttocks, sinking down low with your feet flat on the floor.

POINTS

Move at a slow, even speed. • Imagine you are a bird, spreading its wings, folding its wings, and finally settling down on water. This will help you to get the right "feeling." • Breathe naturally.

HORSE STANCE TURNING

1 Assume a horse-riding stance. Feel really solid.

2 Place your hands on your thighs, thumbs pointing toward your back. Stand straight.

3 Lean over to your left knee, back straight.

4 Then circle the body horizontally toward your right knee.

5 Rise up into a vertical position and repeat the movement to the right side.

POINTS

At first lean only a little way forward until you become accustomed to the exercise. • Try to use only the muscles needed, in your back. • Keep your back relatively straight with your head and neck in line with the back.

CRANE BALANCING

1 Stand up straight.

2 Raise your right thigh to a horizontal position and lift your arms to the side to help your balance. Hold for 5-10 seconds.

3 In one movement, bend forward at your waist and place your right foot, sole flat on the floor, behind you.

4 Let your arms hang down in front of you in this position and relax your chest muscles. Hold for 5 seconds.

5 Rise straight up into the thigh-raised position. Continue and from time to time alternate the legs.

POINTS

Move at your own chosen speed.
• Try to hold the positions without wobbling. • In the leaning forward position, keep your rear leg, buttocks, back, neck, and head in one relatively straight line. Do not push your buttocks up into the air. • This exercise will help you to do the movements of the Form which require balancing on one leg. It will also enable you to feel comfortable when using only one leg for support, and give you a clear impression of one leg being empty, yin, and other one being full, yang.

REACHING THE SKY AND TOUCHING THE EARTH

1 Stand in a normal position, feet directly under your hips.

2 Turn your palm toward the front and then lift them diagonally forward.

3 When your palms are high up in front and above you, turn them over.

4 Your fingers should be pointing toward one another, but not touching. Gently press down.

5 When your palms reach just below your navel, turn them outward again and repeat the exercise.

POINTS

Relax and breathe naturally.
• Imagine that you are in a pleasant rural setting with fresh air and the scent of flowers or pine trees. As you lift your arms, the beauty and energy of Nature floods into your arms and upper body. As you lower your arms, this energy flows down into your lower body, legs, and feet. Do this exercise without forcing. Imagine that a gentle breeze flows into and through you, eliminating unquiet thoughts.

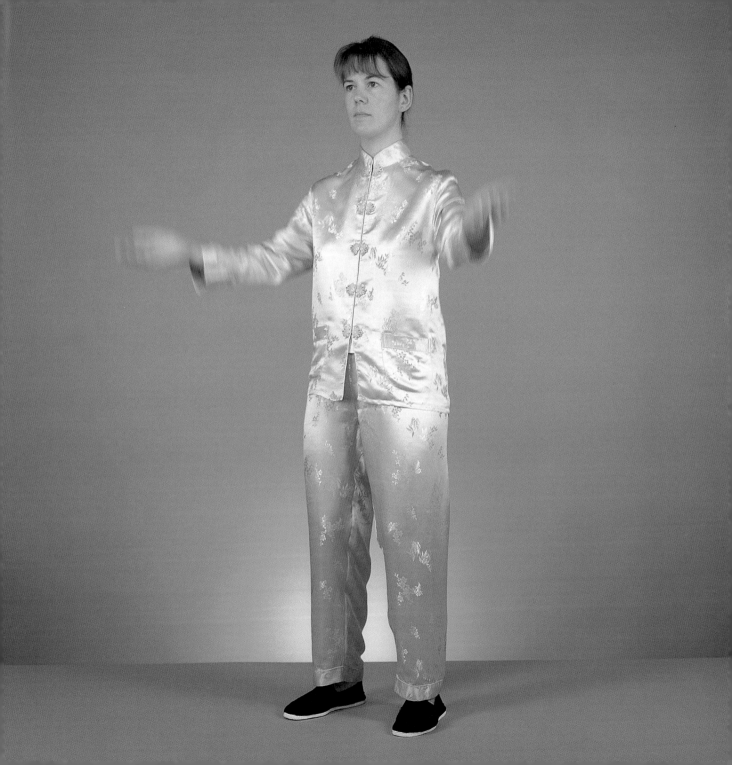

1 Stand with your feet slightly wider apart than your hips.

2 Relax and wait for a minute until you feel "settled." Bring your arms in a wide circle out to the sides.

3 Then bring your arms in front as if holding a big ball. Your palms face your chest, thumbs up, fingertips about 2 inches apart.

4 Gaze horizontally into the middle distance for three minutes. Slowly bring your palms closer to your body...

5 ... and without touching it "brush" down to your lower abdomen. Bring your arms to the sides.

POINTS

Let your elbows hang lower than your palms. Relax your chest and pectoral muscles, letting your shoulders sink to their natural position. • This exercise is done after all the others to allow your body to calm down and to focus, prior to beginning the Form. If you do these exercises before you begin the Form, you will feel more prepared for it. Holding a Ball is one of many Chi Kung (Qi Gong) exercises for cultivating energy. Tai Chi Chuan itself can be studied as a Chi Kung exercise, but the Form is often long and complex. Chi Kung is best left until you have more experience.

THE FORM

The Form is described as if you were standing in the middle of a compass, facing South. In Chinese culture, South is regarded as the direction of warmth and good fortune. The Form is meant to be done from the first movement through to the last, but you may of course practice individual movements.

As with all Forms, you will come across variations. This does not mean that any presentation is "wrong." It simply means that the physical movement, when copied, is influenced by the physique, temperament, and Tai Chi background of the teacher or student. If you run across a variation and it appeals to you, adopt it if you wish, provided it does not obviously go against the basic principles – in which case, "stick to your guns."

When doing the Form, it is traditional to face South.

In the illustrations where the performer turns his back, smaller illustrations have been inset to show the positions from the other side. Also, in a few places, arrows have been inserted to show the direction of the hand movements. These arrows show HOW TO REACH THE NEXT POSITION, but the caption instructions are placed UNDER THAT NEXT POSITION.

BOW STANCE

1

sThe most common completed stance in the Form is the Bow Stance. The front foot points directly forward.

2

The rear foot points out at approximately 45 degrees to the front foot. The rear foot is *never behind* the front foot, always to the side and rear.

1

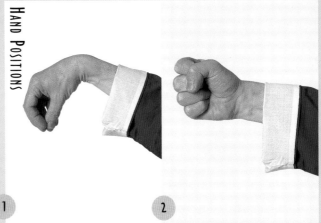

1   **2**

Unless otherwise stated, both feet are placed and kept flat on the floor during a movement. Do not sway or rock.

The "Beak" formation is made by bending the wrist lightly and bringing the tips of the fingers and thumbs together.

The fist is formed with the thumb on the outside of the fingers, lightly clenched.

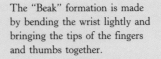

2

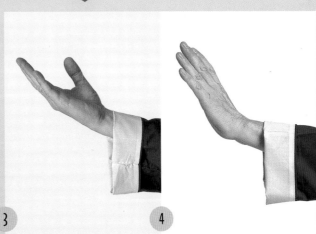

3   **4**

When the instructions tell you to raise the toes, lift the whole foot except for the heel.

In general, during the movement from one completed posture to another, the hands are in this more relaxed, Yin, shape. Energy (*Chi*) is collected.

As a movement comes to completion, the hands flex a little into this more Yang shape. Energy (*Chi*) is sent out.

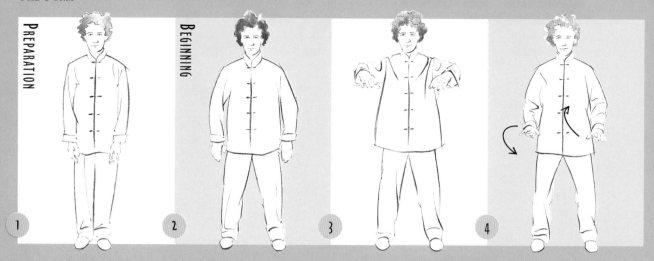

1

Stand in a relaxed posture, heels close together, arms hanging naturally, eyes level with the horizon and looking into the middle distance.

BEGINNING

2

Step to your left with the left foot, making the feet parallel. Take your arms a few inches from your body and turn the palms to face the rear.

3

Raise your arms in front of you to shoulder level, elbows slightly bent outward, palms down.

4

Bring your elbows down, closer to your body and lower your palms to hip level.

9

Step left into the Bow Stance, pressing down with your right palm and raising your left palm in front of you.

PART WILD HORSE MANE – 2

10

Shift your weight back onto the right leg and raise your left toes, turning your waist right; "hold a ball" on the right side, right hand on top.

11

Turn left, keeping your left toes raised, and "hold a ball" on the left side, left hand on top.

12

Shift your weight onto your left foot, and bring your right foot close to it, heel raised.

HOLD THE BALL

PART WILD HORSE MANE — 1

5
Raise your left hand a few inches and lower your right hand a few inches, turning your waist a little to the left.

6
Raise your right hand a few inches and lower your left hand a few inches, turning your waist a little to the right.

7
Bring your left foot, heel raised, closer to your right foot and "hold a ball" on the right side, right hand on top.

8
Turn right on the ball of your left foot and look toward your left (East).

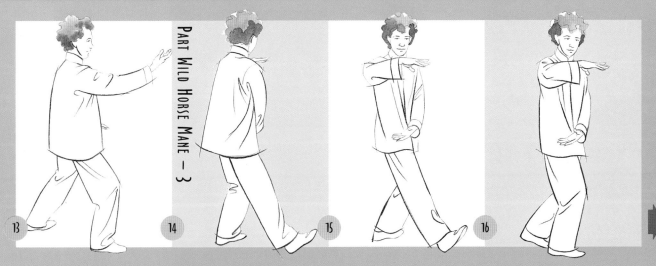

PART WILD HORSE MANE — 3

13
Step directly East with your right foot into a Bow Stance and Part Wild Horse Mane again, as in movement No. 9, on the opposite side.

14
Shift your weight back onto your left leg and raise your right toes, turning your waist left; "hold the ball" on the left side, left hand on top.

15
Turn right, keeping your right heel raised, and "hold a ball" on the right side, right hand on top.

16
Shift your weight onto your right foot, and bring your left foot close to it, heel raised.

WHITE CRANE SPREADS ITS WINGS

17 Step directly East with your left foot into a Bow Stance and Part Wild Horse Mane again, as in movement No. 9.

18 Slide your right foot forward a few inches, heel raised, weight mainly on left foot; and make as if to "hold a ball," left hand on top.

19 Settle your weight back onto your right foot, turn your waist to the right, raising your right hand and lowering the left.

20 Turn your waist left to face directly East, lifting your right hand diagonally forward opposite your right temple, and lower your left palm beside your left thigh.

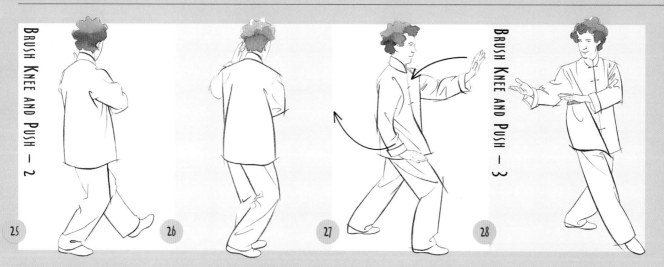

BRUSH KNEE AND PUSH — 2

25 Shift weight and raise your left toes. Turn waist left. Raise your left palm, facing up, level with your chin. "Point" your right fingers at your left elbow joint.

26 Step up with your right foot, close to the left, heel raised. Begin to "brush" across your waist with your right hand, palm down, and push forward with your left palm.

27 Step directly to the East with your right foot into a Bow Stance and complete the "brush" and push.

BRUSH KNEE AND PUSH — 3

28 Shift your weight back onto your left foot and turn your right foot out, toes slightly raised.

BRUSH KNEE AND PUSH – 1

21 Turn your left foot inward. Lower your right palm down and raise the left, palm up. Look back over your right shoulder.

22 Turn your right foot out. Continue to lower your right palm, then raise it, facing up; at the same time, your left palm circles down across your chest.

23 Your weight shifts to your right leg: you swivel to face East, left heel raised. Your right hand continues to rise, level with your ear.

24 Step directly East, turning your whole body. Your left palm "brushes" above your left knee, and your right hand pushes forward.

PLAY GUITAR

29 Step up with your left foot, heel raised, close to the right and start the "brush" and push actions again.

30 Step directly East into a Bow Stance and complete the "brush" and push actions. *In all these movements, let your waist and trunk lead and your arms follow.*

31 Sometimes known as "Jade Girl Strums The Lute"! Draw your right foot closer to the left, heel raised and lower both hands, palms down.

32 Shift your weight onto your right foot, and raise your left heel. Bend both wrists and "point" your fingers downward a little.

STEP BACK TO DRIVE MONKEY AWAY – 1

33 Raise your left leg about a foot from the floor, knee bent, then place the heel down, at the same time lifting your hands into a kind of guitar-holding position.

34 Lower your right hand past your thighs and raise it, palm up, level with your shoulder. Stretch your left hand forward, palm down. Look at your right palm.

35 Bring right palm close to your ear, and pull left hand back toward your thigh, palm up. Draw your left foot close to the right, heel raised. Move West, facing East.

36 Step directly backward with your left foot and shift your weight on to it, pushing forward with your right hand and pulling your left hand beside your left thigh.

STEP BACK TO DRIVE MONKEY AWAY – 4

41 Draw your left foot back close to the right, heel raised. Bring your right palm close to your right ear and your left palm, facing up, toward your left thigh.

42 Step directly backward, West, with your left foot, pushing forward with your right hand and bringing your left palm, facing up, beside your left thigh.

43 Turn to look at your left hand as it rises, palm up, level with your shoulder. At the same time, straighten your right wrist and turn your palm up.

44 Draw your right foot close to the left, heel raised, and bring your left palm close to your left ear. Draw your right palm back, palm up, toward your right thigh.

STEP BACK TO DRIVE MONKEY AWAY – 2

STEP BACK TO DRIVE MONKEY AWAY – 3

Raise your left hand, palm up, level with your shoulder. Turn your right palm upward. Turn your waist to look at your left hand.

Draw back your right foot to the left, heel raised. Bring your left hand beside your left ear and draw your right hand, palm up, toward your right thigh.

Step directly backward with your right foot, shifting your weight on to it. Push forward with your left hand and bring your right hand, palm up, beside your right thigh.

Turn your waist to the right, raising your right hand, palm up. Straighten out your right wrist, before turning the palm up. Look at your right hand.

WARD OFF LEFT

ROLL BACK

Step directly backward with your right foot, pushing forward with your left palm and pulling your right palm, facing up, beside your right thigh.

Turn your waist to the right, bringing your left foot close to your right foot, heel raised. "Hold a ball" on your right side, your right hand on top.

Step forward, East, into a Bow Stance with your left foot. Raise your left arm in a curve across your body. Press down with your right hand beside your right thigh.

Turn your waist left, raising your left palm to point up and bringing your right palm, facing up, below and to the side of your left forearm.

PRESS

PUSH

49 Roll back by shifting your weight onto your right leg, lowering your right arm and bringing your left arm over toward your chest.

50 Place your right fingers on your left pulse, turning your waist to face East once more.

51 Shift your weight forward into a Bow Stance and extend your arms ahead of your body, keeping your elbows slightly bent.

52 Slide your right palm, facing down, over your left palm, facing down, and begin to shift your weight back onto your right leg.

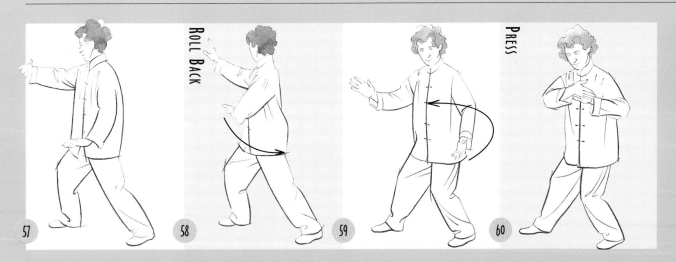

ROLL BACK

PRESS

57 Step directly West into a Bow Stance, raising your right arm to chest height, your palm facing your body and pressing down with your left palm.

58 Turn your waist to the right. Raise your right palm, facing away, and cup your left palm to move to the side of and below your right forearm.

59 Roll back by shifting your weight onto your left leg, lowering your left palm as you turn your waist left and bringing your right palm in front of your body.

60 Place the fingers of your left hand on the pulse of the right as you draw your arms closer to your body to turn to face West.

WARD OFF RIGHT

53 Shift your weight back on to your right leg and draw your elbows down to the sides of your chest, palms pointing up and facing away from your body.

54 Shift your weight on to your left leg in a Bow Stance, extend your arms into a Push and keep your elbows slightly bent.

55 Shift your weight back onto your right foot, and turn inward on your left heel into an inward-turned stance. Wipe your hands horizontally to the right.

56 Begin to bring your weight mainly onto your left leg and slide your right foot closer to the left, "holding a ball" on the left side.

PUSH

61 Shift your weight into a Bow Stance, weight on your right foot, and extend your arms ahead of your chest, facing directly West.

62 Slide your left palm, facing down, over your right hand, palm facing down and start to move your weight back onto your left foot.

63 "Sit down" on your left leg and drop your elbows to the sides of your chest, palms facing away from your body, fingers pointing up.

64 Shift your weight onto your right leg in a Bow Stance and push ahead away from your body, elbows slightly bent.

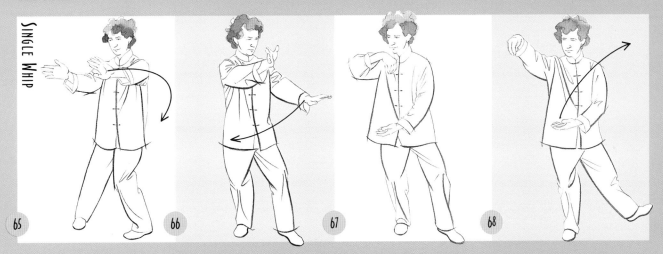

SINGLE WHIP

65 Move your weight onto your left leg, as your waist turns left and your right foot swivels inward on the heel. Wipe your hands horizontally to the right.

66 Shift your weight onto your right leg, and raise your left heel as you swivel on the ball of the foot. Push your right hand ahead as your left palm descends.

67 Draw your right hand close to the right side of the chest and make a "beak," fingers and thumb tips touching. Lower your left hand under the "beak."

68 Step directly East with your left heel, pushing the "beak" out to the side and back.

73 Raise your left palm, facing your body, and lower your right. Complete bringing your right foot parallel to the left.

74 Turn your waist and trunk to the left and in doing so take your arms to the left side of your body. There should be no independent arm movement.

75 At the moment you complete this turning, slide your right foot inward closer to the left foot.

76 Begin to raise your right hand and lower the left, turning your waist right, to the front (South).

WAVE HANDS IN CLOUDS

69 Begin to shift your weight onto your right foot, raising your left palm diagonally upward across the abdomen and chest until it faces your head.

70 Shift your weight into a Bow Stance, pushing directly East with your left palm. Swivel your right foot inward slightly on the heel.

71 Swivel right on your left heel as you shift your weight onto your right foot. Open your right palm and bring your left palm down beside your left thigh.

72 Shift your weight onto your left foot, drawing your right foot alongside it. Turn and look right as you pull your right arm so that the palm faces West.

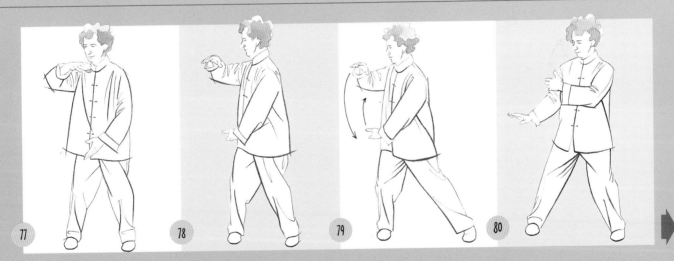

77 Continue to turn to the right with your right hand at neck height and the left in front of your lower abdomen.

78 Complete the rightward turn and look to the right, your weight on your right foot.

79 Step away to the left with your left foot. The feet are always parallel throughout this movement.

80 Begin to raise your left hand and lower the right, shifting your weight onto your left foot.

SINGLE WHIP

81 Complete the raising of your left hand and lowering of the right, beginning to turn to face front (South).

82 Complete the turn to the left.

83 Step diagonally forward to your right a few inches with your right foot. Make a "beak" with your right hand and cup your left palm under it.

84 Step a little to the left with your left foot, on the heel, and draw your left palm, facing your neck, in front of you.

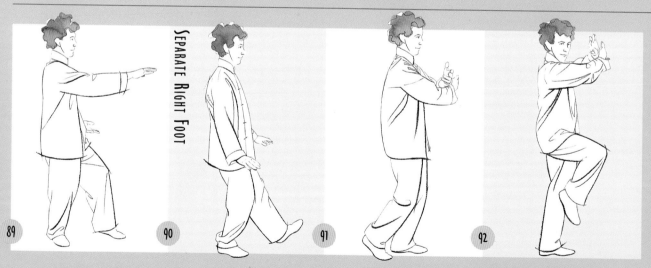

SEPARATE RIGHT FOOT

89 Continue to push your right hand forward and pull the left back into the positions shown.

90 Step onto your left heel and lower your hands, palms down, beside your thighs.

91 Shift your weight onto your left leg and raise your right heel. Cross your hands over at your lower forearms and raise them in front of your chest.

92 Raise your arms in front of your neck, and lift your right knee. Toes point down. Turn your trunk to face Southeast (right diagonal), palms face out.

HIGH PAT ON HORSE

85 Turn to the left and bring your left hand in front of your face, beginning to shift your weight onto your right foot.

86 Shift your weight into a Bow Stance, weight on your left foot, and push your left hand ahead of your face, facing directly East.

87 Begin to draw your left foot back toward the right, heel raised, opening out your right palm, turning your left palm up and looking at your right hand.

88 Draw your left foot back, heel raised, and push your right hand forward, palm down. At the same time, bring your left hand down. Weight is on right foot.

STRIKE WITH BOTH FISTS

93 Kick out with your right foot, slowly, and separate your arms at shoulder height. Point your toes.

94 Swivel on your left foot so that your whole body faces directly Southeast. Bring both palms, facing down, in front of your body at shoulder height.

95 Raise your right knee a little higher and clench both fists lightly, palms facing your body, held vertically.

96 Step forward with your right foot onto the heel and slowly swing your arms down and then out to the sides.

SEPARATE LEFT FOOT

97 Shift your weight forward into a Bow Stance, weight on your right foot, and "strike" to the temples of an imaginary opponent. Move slowly as always.

98 Shift your weight onto your left leg as you turn left, turning your right foot inward on the heel and lowering your hands, palms facing inward.

99 Continue to turn left. Shift your weight back onto right foot and swivel further around on your right heel, then on the left. Cross hands in front of your waist.

100 Raise your hands to neck height, turning them away from your body, and raise your left knee, toes pointing down.

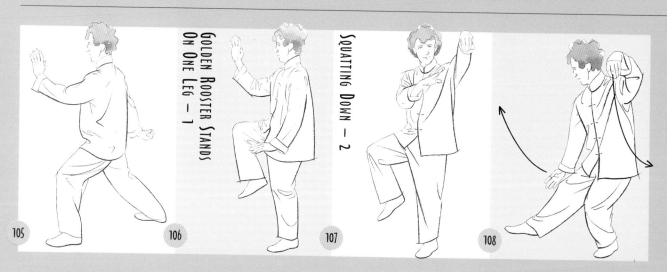

GOLDEN ROOSTER STANDS ON ONE LEG – 1

SQUATTING DOWN – 2

105 Move into a completed Bow Stance, raising your left palm vertically upward in front of your face and hook behind you with the "beak" of your right hand.

106 Raise right knee so that thigh is parallel with the floor. Press down to thigh level with left hand and thrust upward with a vertical right palm, facing inward.

107 Begin to lower your right leg, swivel a little to the left, making a "beak" with your left hand, at shoulder height, and "point" your right fingers toward it.

108 Place your right foot on the floor and make a thrust downward with your right hand along the side of your thigh.

SQUATTING DOWN — 1

101 Kick out to the Northwest with your left foot, separating your hands at shoulder height.

102 Make a "beak" with your right hand and point your left fingers at it, palm down. Bend your left knee. NOTE see No. 107.

103 Step directly West with your left foot and begin to sweep your left palm down in front of your body.

104 Shift your weight onto your left leg and push your left palm forward.

GOLDEN ROOSTER STANDS ON ONE LEG — 2

FAIR LADY WORKS SHUTTLES

109 Shift your weight onto your right leg to make a Bow Stance, thrusting upward vertically with your right palm and hooking back with the "beak" of your left palm.

110 Raise your left knee so that your thigh is parallel with the floor, thrusting up with your left palm, vertically and bringing your right palm down.

111 Step down to your left front with the left heel and bring your right palm in front of your abdomen, facing in. Your left palm is raised beside the left side of your head.

112 Shift your weight fully onto your left leg and raise your right heel, while both palms "hold a ball" on the left side of your body, left palm on top.

Step to the Northwest with your right foot; raise your right arm, palm facing your body, pushing forward across your chest with your vertical left palm.

Shift your weight fully into a Bow Stance, Northwest, raising your right hand above your head and pushing forward at chin height with your vertical left palm.

Ease your weight back onto your left leg. Your left palm faces up, cupped below your right elbow as you lower it in front of your chest.

Lower your arms a little farther as you shift your weight onto your right leg and draw your left foot up behind it.

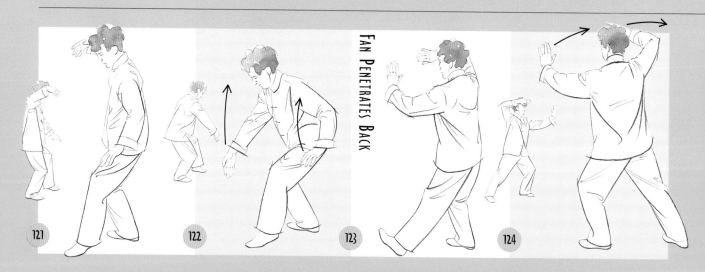

FAN PENETRATES BACK

Turn your waist back to the left, raising your right palm up beside your head and lowering your left palm down toward the outside of your left thigh. Look down.

Thrust down with your right palm, facing inward. Pull your left palm beside your left thigh and "sit down" on your rear leg, bending forward.

Rise up with weight mainly on right leg. Step directly West. Raise your right hand, palm facing out, and your left hand in front of your face.

Shift your weight into a Bow Stance, directly West, and push ahead with your left palm.

Step toward the Southwest with your left heel, bringing your left hand in front of your chest and pushing across your chest with your vertical right palm.

Shift your weight into a Bow Stance, raising your left hand in front of and above your head. Push forward with your vertical right palm.

Draw your right leg in closer to the left, with the heel raised. Begin to press down equally with both palms.

Shift weight back onto right leg, turning to the right. Lower your left palm down across your chest, and raise right palm. Your left heel is slightly raised.

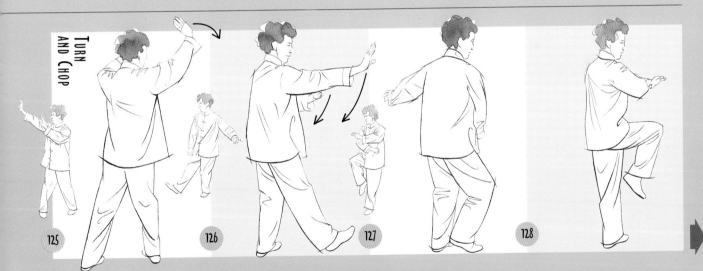

TURN AND CHOP

Shift your weight onto your right foot and turn your left foot inward, swiveling on your heel. Circle both of your hands over your head.

Shift your weight back onto your left foot and turn out your right foot, swiveling on your heel, toes raised. Press down with both palms. Facing East.

Draw your right foot back to the left, heel raised. Take your left arm out to your left side. Make a light fist with your right hand. Draw it in front of your abdomen.

Raise your right knee, thigh parallel with the floor, toes down. Raise your right fist up to your chest as you press down with your left palm.

PARRY AND PUNCH

129 Step forward with your right foot, onto the heel, and strike (slowly) with the back of your right fist at an imaginary opponent's face.

130 Turn out your right foot and shift your weight onto it. Push forward with your vertical left palm and draw your right fist back to your hip, lightly clenched.

131 Step forward with your left foot, onto the heel. Begin to bring your right fist forward and to bend your left arm.

132 Shift your weight onto your left foot to make a Bow Stance and punch slowly horizontally forward, bring your vertical left palm beside your right forearm.

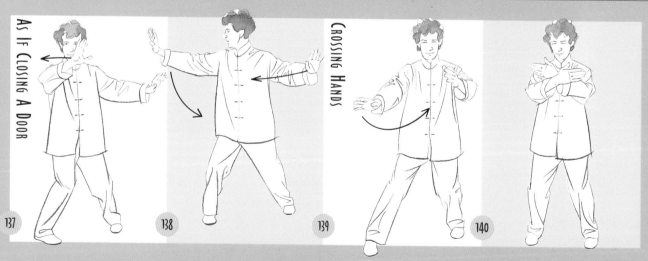

AS IF CLOSING A DOOR

CROSSING HANDS

137 Shift your weight to your right leg. Turn right and turn your left foot inward, swiveling on the heel. Push your right hand out to front (South) at face level.

138 Begin to shift your weight back onto your left leg, swiveling your right foot right on the heel. Push your right palm out far right.

139 Move your weight onto your left leg and sweep your right palm inward toward the center of your body as your left palm does the same.

140 Draw your right leg back, parallel with the left (face South as at the very beginning). Cross both hands in front of your upper chest, right farthest from your body.

WITHDRAW AND PUSH

Slide your left hand, palm down, under your right upper arm as you turn your right palm upward and open. Begin to move weight back slowly onto your right foot.

Turn your left palm upward and separate both hands so that the fingers point directly in front of you. Your weight continues to move back onto your right leg.

With your weight mainly on your right leg, lower your elbows to the sides of your chest.

Shift your weight into a left Bow Stance and push horizontally forward with both vertical palms.

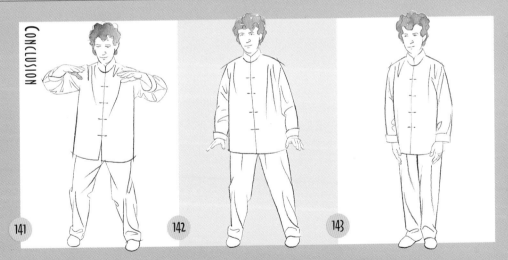

CONCLUSION

Draw both hands apart to the sides of your upper chest.

Lower your palms to the sides of your thighs and look at the horizon, middle distance.

Bring your left foot back to the right, heels close together and lower your palms to a natural position beside your thighs.

RELAX... JUST RELAX

SPECIFIC APPLICATIONS

Most people take their bodies for granted. As a rule, it is only when their attention is involuntarily drawn to it, through injury, illness, or in the case of women, pregnancy, that they focus on their bodies. In Chinese eyes, this is a typical Western attitude. A Chinese physician is someone who helps a person to stay well; in the West, people resort to a doctor to make them better. If you think about it, the Chinese approach is the more sensible one.

Tai Chi is part of the Chinese system of keeping well. The following section describes some of the benefits which the art bestows on its students. Some of them are curative and some preventive. They are based on knowledge derived from Traditional Chinese Medicine, and the application of that knowledge over several centuries to the specific movements of Tai Chi. The benefits of Tai Chi are interdependent. You cannot have one without the other. As you read more about the subject, and then as you train and study, this will become apparent.

HEAD AND NECK

The relationship between head and neck can be vastly improved through the correct performance of Tai Chi. The head is "carried" by the neck.

STRESS

Stress is all about trying to do something about something at the wrong time. To do Tai Chi well, you have to live in the present moment, where there is no stress.

HEAD AND SPINE

The head should be a "free" extension of the spine. This means that it can work in concert with the vertebrae, but also independently.

CORRECT JOINT USE

As you perform Tai Chi, you inevitably learn the correct use of most of the joints of the body. You may even begin to wonder why you never discovered it for yourself.

OTHER BENEFITS

Tai Chi can produce a previously unknown feeeling of calm, associated with the peace of natural scenes, softly swaying grasses, and placid lakes.

CIRCULATION

Tai Chi is the best form of exercise for improving circulation of energy and *Chi*. After some time, you should feel the benefits in the hands and feet.

DIGESTION

Tai Chi is meant to relax the body, uniformly, and to distribute the energy, uniformly. This soothes the body and helps to promote better digestion.

OLDER PEOPLE

No one has yet discovered a cure for old age, but Tai Chi can defeat the growing immobility which afflicts elderly people. Can millions of Chinese be wrong?

MUSCLE TONE

The tone of the muscles should be neither too Yin nor too Yang; that is, Optimum, the best there is. Prolonged training can produce this happy state of affairs.

BALANCE

Correct Tai Chi training should improve your balance and banish the deep-seated fear of falling. You begin to feel solidly rooted on the earth.

HEAD AND NECK

The neck is a very important area of the body. Problems with the vertebrae, muscles, and nerves in this area can cause stiffness, pain, headaches, and tension.

JOINTS

Joints (see page 53) not only allow us to move the way we do, but also facilitate the flow of blood and *Chi*. However, incorrectly used, they can impede this flow. If you lift your chin high, you can feel the bones and muscles at the back of the neck contract and close together. You don't need any medical knowledge to realize that this position blocks the flow of energy through the region. This is an extreme example, since you cannot help but be aware of the tension. However, most people have a lot of unrecognized and unnecessary tension in this part of the body, which affects their feeling of well–being.

CHI AND ENERGY

In Chinese terms, this blocking of energy means that the *Chi* and the blood are not able to flow naturally from the body, into the head, and back down into the body. At the point where the tension begins, there is an excess (stagnancy) of *Chi*, and at the point where the tension ends there is a deficit of *Chi*. This pattern of excess – stagnancy – deficiency is a basic principle of Traditional Chinese Medicine.

Balance your head and look life quietly in the face . . .

BREATHING

This new relationship between the head and the neck is not easy to attain. But if you practice Tai Chi regularly, you will reach it. One of the benefits, in addition to the flow of energy, is that breathing will tend to deepen. If the muscles of the neck region are too contracted, the chest cannot rise and fall as well as it might, and breathing action will be restricted.

As the head begins to float up, the chest will sink, the rib cage becomes free, and the abdomen begins to take part in breathing. When you start experiencing this new, deeper breathing, which should come naturally and not be forced in any way, you will begin to realize that "breath is life" and that breathing correctly increases your energy, reduces stress, and helps you sleep.

Once you know some of the Form (pages 26–45) well, it is a good idea to go through it specifically focusing on letting your head "float" up, while giving less attention to the other movements. To help yourself in this direction, try to relax your forehead and orbits of the eyes. Release your jaw and let the chin drop down a little.

A word of warning: it is not possible to isolate one part of the body from another and what is said in this section should be combined with the information and advice given elsewhere in the book.

DEEP, UNFORCED BREATHING

BREATHING IN
the ribs stretch and semi-straighten the diaphragm

BREATHING OUT
the diaphragm is raised as the pressure is released

lungs

diaphragm

Deep, unforced breathing can give you a new feeling about yourself. Diaphragm and chest muscles work in harmony.

ALTERNATIVE REMEDIES

Acupuncture, acupressure, and herbal remedies are all ways of bringing the *Chi* back into balance. Tai Chi has its own healing formula of relaxation, gentle movement, and working toward the posture of "head suspended from above as if by a single hair." The sensation to aim for when doing The Form is one of the head being lightly carried on the top of the spine; the head floating up, while the rest of the body sinks down (see also pages 50 and 55).

HEAD AND SPINE

Western, as well as Chinese, healers have recognized the importance of the occiput to health. This is the place where the skull rests on the top of the spine. Bad posture means that the neck muscles are unnecessarily contracted, impeding the flow of the *Chi* and causing tension and potential back problems as well as shallow breathing.

Tai Chi places great emphasis on correct posture. The Tai Chi maxim states that the head should be suspended above the vertebrae as if held by a single hair. Although this floating posture is not physically attainable, try to move toward such a goal.

Do not crunch your head onto your neck.

POSTURE

Children naturally have good posture, but bad habits form as we grow older. Often a particular way of standing or holding the head becomes a habit, placing strain on vertebrae and muscles, and causing stress and potential damage. The head becomes jammed down onto the spine like a tight hat, bent back, or hung forward. It is rarely in the optimum position of the Chinese maxim.

CHI

The Tai Chi saying that the *Chi* must go down implies that it must also at some stage go up. According to Tai Chi theory, the *Chi* descends down the front of the body along one of the major channels and ascends up the spine, over the top of the head, and down again. Congestion in the occipital region hinders this flow.

Tai Chi training, with its emphasis on letting the head float up naturally, focuses on the vertebrae, training the spine to fall into a more natural position and bringing the entire body into alignment.

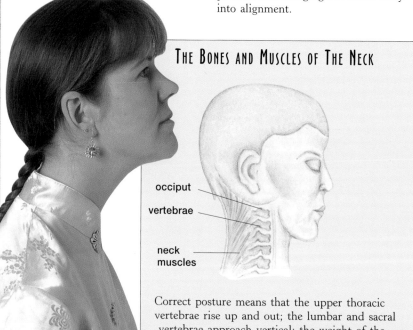

THE BONES AND MUSCLES OF THE NECK

occiput

vertebrae

neck muscles

Correct posture means that the upper thoracic vertebrae rise up and out; the lumbar and sacral vertebrae approach vertical; the weight of the front of the body is supported by the spine and the flow of energy through the body is unimpeded. This, in turn, has a beneficial effect on circulation (see opposite).

CIRCULATION

Everyone knows that good blood circulation is important. Oxygen, nutrients, carbon dioxide, and waste products depend on it. Closely allied with circulation are heart rate and breathing. Traditional Chinese Medicine carries this a stage further and adds that these functions of the body depend on an optimum supply of *Chi* – neither too much, nor too little. The *Chi* helps the circulation of the blood.

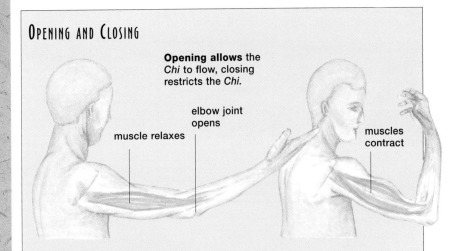

OPENING AND CLOSING

Opening allows the *Chi* to flow, closing restricts the *Chi.*

muscle relaxes

elbow joint opens

muscles contract

The action of Opening and Closing (see page 13) directs the circulation to the tips of the toes and fingers, reducing cold in the extremities. Indeed, Tai Chi students often experience tingling in feet and hands caused by the circulation being stimulated. In Chinese terms, this tingling indicates the activity of the *Chi.*

Lifestyle, of course, strongly influences circulation. A fixed routine, for instance, results in an established and repetitive circulation. In contrast, a hectic pace of life means that the restorative part of the nervous system has little chance to operate. In both cases, traditional Chinese medicine sees Tai Chi as a means of bringing the circulation into balance.

With its slow, even pace, Tai Chi stimulates the restorative powers of the body when you are neither asleep nor resting. From one point of view, the movements are like a slow self-massage without hands! When the muscles are trained to relax, they move easily from relaxation to tension and back again pumping the venous blood and lymphatic fluid back toward the heart and lungs in a steady, even way.

In time, breathing will deepen (see page 49) as you learn to use the diaphragm muscles to greater effect, thus improving the intake of oxygen. Your heart rate will become more regular and even slower. And you will notice that the recovery back to your normal heart rate after exercise will take less time.

Once again, you can see that everything in Tai Chi is linked together and that it is impossible to isolate any one element.

MUSCLE TONE

As far as health is concerned, it is preferable to have what is called good muscle tone rather than strength. Muscles can be very soft and flabby, yin, or hard as iron, yang. Good tone is somewhere in between these two extremes: a condition in which the very small elements that make up a muscle are at their "happiest." In this condition, they are best able to relax more or to tense more, whatever is required.

Tai Chi cultivates smoothness of action, and this is what muscles in general like. Muscles work in a two-way fashion. When the biceps flex in the upper arm, the triceps extend in the upper arm. The biceps are the agonist muscles when they cause the arm to bend, and the triceps are the antagonist muscles. When the arm is straightened, the two muscle groups reverse their roles. Without an antagonist muscle, the action of the agonist muscle could not be controlled.

So smoothness of action means that the relation between the two muscle groups is optimum. In an ideal situation, all the muscle groups of the body would synchronize harmoniously, and the resulting benefit to the body would be incredible.

When a muscle stretches, there is a built-in tendency for it to want to go back in the opposite direction. This is called a stretch reflex. Interestingly, it is in harmony with a fundamental principle of the yin-yang theory. This propounds that when any phenomenon reaches its maximum yin or yang condition, it naturally begins to move in the opposite direction.

When you move in haste, there is no time to think about your muscles or about the effect the movement may have on them. In Tai Chi there is ample time to get in tune with your body and to listen to what it is telling you.

Learning the Form is like learning to play a musical instrument – your first efforts will be clumsy and uncoordinated. However, once you have acquired skill, you are able to produce fine differences in tone and volume. Likewise, once you know the basic movements of the Form, you will be able to fine-tune your actions so that muscle tone, smoothness of movement, awareness of flex, reflex, and feedback all combine harmoniously. This is an ideal condition for the flow of *Chi*.

If you make Tai Chi part of your daily life, you will find that concentrating on this harmony of movement will firm up your muscles and improve your level of fitness.

Other forms of gentle exercise such as cycling, walking, and swimming can be very beneficial for muscle tone.

CORRECT JOINT USE

Good muscle tone can work in harmony with correct use of the joints. Because we are not generally as closely in touch with our physical activity as animals are, we are not nearly as aware of what they are doing. We often misuse our joints, compelling them to move in ways for which they are not designed.

In Traditional Chinese Medicine, the joints are very important because they facilitate or impede the flow of *Chi* (see page 9).

Correct use as taught in Tai Chi will help to correct any *Chi* imbalance and improve stiff joints.

KNEE AND ANKLE JOINTS

The knee and ankle joints are ideal for illustrating joint use. Both are hinge joints, working more or less like the hinge of a door. This means that when you bend your knee and ankle, the knee should move forward over the foot. If you stand up and look down at your feet, then bend your knees, you should lose sight of your feet. If your knees move outward or your lower leg falls inward, this is wrong and places a strain on the joints.

In Tai Chi there is a maxim which says that the knee should not extend beyond the toes. This means that the knee should be over the foot in the first place, and that to avoid strain on the knee, it should not extend beyond the toes.

The fleet-footed cheetah knows all about correct joint use.

ELBOW JOINT

The elbow is also a hinge joint, but at the top of the forearm there is another joint which enables it to rotate. In Tai Chi, both of these joints are fully used, and the maxim that the elbows should be down is incorporated into the Form. Keeping the elbows down means that the shoulder joints are not in a constant state of tension holding the whole arms up. This in turn means that there is less strain on the chest, which leads to greater ease of breathing.

WRIST JOINT

The wrist joint is more complex. It can act like a hinge, rotate, and also turn from side to side. If you go more deeply into Tai Chi, you will learn how to use the wrist joint in combination with the extending and contracting of the palm.

DIGESTION

Traditional Chinese Medicine says that human beings contain a number of vital energies and substances. These are *Shen* (spirit), *Jing* (vital energy released), *Chi* (intrinsic energy), blood (blood and the functions of blood), and fluids (sweat, urine). *Shen* is the finest; fluids are the coarsest.

Fresh fruits and vegetables are not only good for the digestive system, but for our overall health.

These five are linked together in an ascending chain. *Shen* is the highest product. If there is anything wrong with any of them, then the whole chain is disrupted. This is true in the eyes of Western medicine, too. If there is something wrong with any organ of digestion and elimination, then the whole body will be affected.

Beginning with the mouth, it is traditional in Tai Chi to keep the tip of the tongue lightly in contact with the roof of the mouth behind the teeth. This stimulates the flow of saliva, which is swallowed slowly. The calm feeling accompanying Tai Chi helps to "comfort" the stomach and other organs which contribute to good digestion.

The regular breathing and slow, even body movement "massage" the organs and help to regulate their activity. And the ordered *Chi* flow contributes the energy necessary for their good functioning.

The liver is regarded as a very important organ in Traditional Chinese Medicine. Certain

Single Whip done with the left arm leading – is said to be particularly beneficial to the liver.

Traditional Chinese Medicine says that human beings contain a number of vital energies and substances.

movements of the Form – for instance, Single Whip (page 36), done with the left arm leading – are said to be particularly beneficial to the liver. *It is not advisable, except under the guidance of a knowledgeable teacher, to perform single repetitions of a movement to attain a particular benefit.* Step Back To Drive Monkey Away (page 32) is said to benefit kidney function, especially in women.

Finally, Tai Chi can be very beneficial for constipation. The overall feeling generated by the Form induces the large intestine to return to normal, and the movements themselves seem to aid peristalsis.

BALANCE

It is not an exaggeration to say that many people are, to a large extent, cut off from the sensations of abdomen and legs. They do not experience that they are on the earth – quite literally. Small wonder then that if they feel they may lose their balance and fall, they are afraid. They are not sure where they may go if they fall. They are out of touch with what holds them up, their legs.

Tai Chi is sometimes called "meditation in movement." The posture of seated meditation focuses energy in the lower abdomen.

The ideal center of gravity in a standing human being is in the lower abdomen. In Tai Chi, the cultivation of the lower abdomen, its strength and fullness, shows that people in the East have realized for centuries that their health and power reside much lower down than is believed in the West. The posture of seated meditation focuses the energy in this region.

TRAINING

Tai Chi training brings people down to earth. Letting the *Chi* go down, sinking the elbows, bending the knees, placing the feet correctly, and the rest of the Tai Chi maxims all combine to replace the Western emphasis on the upper body with a new one. This is based on simple observation. Gravity keeps human beings glued on the earth, and the nearest contact with gravity is your feet! Tai Chi says that people should build upward from their feet, not downward from their brains. This really makes sense! To carry this sense of gravity a stage further, imagine that you are a tree and that your feet are roots. When a tree is blown by the wind, it bends, yields, but remains in place. This sense of being rooted takes time to acquire. During the first few months of learning Tai Chi, you will need to absorb some of the basic principles of balance mentioned above.

As these principles begin to penetrate your rendering of the Form, you will one day feel, perhaps briefly, that the upper part of your body seems "empty," yin, and the lower part seems "full," yang. When this happens, it is like entering a different world. You have the impression that suddenly you fit into things, into Nature, and that your usual state of mind is one of unnecessary struggling.

If you go on to study Push Hands, training with a partner, you will see that this new condition is an ideal one. When your partner pushes you, your upper body can yield. You do not fall because your lower body is anchored to the ground. Even if you take steps forward or backward, when your feet land, they root to the ground immediately.

STRESS

Stress can be seen partly as a result of overreaction to stimuli of daily life, and partly as a result of the unprecedented pace of modern life. If you are being constantly stimulated by telephone, fax, letters, people, chores, and work pressures, your body and brain do not have time to relax, even if they want to.

Tai Chi, like yoga, is more than just a series of exercises; the body is inextricably linked with the mind. Practicing the Form requires concentration, pushing worries and unrelated thoughts from the mind. Increased physical well-being brings with it a more relaxed state of mind. In time, you will be able to recreate this feeling of relaxation when you are going about your daily life.

Tai Chi can be the dynamic expression of what monks experience in static meditation.

Stress is an attempt to cope with seemingly impossible situations. When you are immersed in them, they seem insoluble. If you can move out of them, you gain a different perspective. Tai Chi is a way of moving out of one situation and into another. The advantage is that you do not have to travel very far – just to your Tai Chi place. The whole focus of your attention moves toward the fundamental things of your life itself. The preoccupations of your mind and emotions become secondary.

If you train regularly at Tai Chi, you have to slow down. Tai Chi demands it. If possible, do your Tai Chi in a natural setting. If this is not possible, find somewhere secluded, at the last resort your bedroom. Train in the same place. This will build up good associations. The place will become a Tai Chi place for you, and when you go there, you will leave behind the demands of life. So much stress centers around an apparent disorder. You struggle to reach some sense of order in a complex of perpetual disorder. In Tai Chi you are taught a natural order, and you try to become one with it. As you gradually succeed, through diligent training and study, you may begin to see the disorder of daily life differently. You may discover that it is not ultimately necessary to be swept away by it. The memory of your Tai Chi times can come back to you, reminding you that a different condition is very close at hand.

MEDITATION IN MOVEMENT

The human brain displays at least five types of wave: *delta* – in deep sleep; *theta* – in light sleep; *alpha* – calm waking state; *beta* – active/stressed state; and *gamma* – fighting pitch. Zen monks' brainwave patterns have been measured during meditation. They move very easily into the *alpha* range and soon afterward into the *theta* range. Experienced Tai Chi students can experience a similar change, which is one of the reasons why Tai Chi is sometimes described as "meditation in movement."

This experience, on a regular basis, can introduce a sense of calm into daily life. However, like most benefits, this does not happen without effort. When doing a simple household or office task, move with the same relaxation and care you bring to the Form. The act of paying attention in a quiet way to some physical activity can move the brain pattern into the *alpha* and possibly toward the *theta*. This does not mean that you fall asleep; if anything, you become more awake. Regular practice will make it easier to recreate this experience of calm in a variety of situations, helping you to take greater control over your emotions and, thus, of your life.

OTHER BENEFITS

Other benefits from Tai Chi are less easily classified, nor are they guaranteed. This is because they require a kind of feedback from the Tai Chi experiences themselves.

For instance, on this page are illustrations of two types of symmetry. The second one is not geometrical, but depends on both the eye of the beholder, and the posture itself. If a dancer or Tai Chi student takes a particular posture and holds it, he or she, or someone looking at him or her, may receive an impression which is very pleasing, esthetically stimulating. If the performer or viewer thinks no more of the experience, then the benefit will be short-lived. If, on the other hand, either of them reflect on it, and start to assume much better postures in daily life, with the benefits which come from that, then the Tai Chi training and daily life will exert a reciprocal influence, and a perennially useful lesson will have been learned.

The symmetry of correct balance and posture.

Obvious, down-the-middle symmetry.

OLDER PEOPLE

As people get older, their health and vitality tends to diminish. How quickly this happens depends on a number of things, but Tai Chi is traditionally regarded as a means of resisting this process. That does not necessarily mean increasing the number of years of one's life, but rather maintaining youthfulness at a higher level than would otherwise have been the case.

Older people discover a new meaning to their lives through the practice of Tai Chi and Chi Kung.

After World War II, the Chinese began investigating the benefits of Tai Chi for the elderly in a more scientific way. They carried out surveys of practitioners of a certain age, comparing them with non-practitioners. In one such project, people aged between 50 and 89 were chosen. The findings showed that, among Tai Chi students, the cardiovascular level was much better, breathing was deeper and more efficient, the strength of the bones and use of the joints was markedly superior, and metabolism in general was well maintained.

Both groups were also asked to step up and down a bench some 14 inches high, and readings were taken of their respiratory and heart functioning. Again, in this set experiment, the Tai Chi group showed a much higher efficiency rate. Both blood pressure and arteriosclerosis were lower. Elasticity of lung tissue and relative movement of the rib cage (which fends off ossification of the rib cartilages) were higher in the Tai Chi group.

It was also discovered that even among the Tai Chi group members who had some ossification of the rib cartilages, which limited the movement of the rib cage, the increased abdominal capacity of the diaphragmatic rise and fall enabled them to breathe "into the abdomen," thereby compensating to some extent.

The spinal columns of the Tai Chi people were more flexible and better aligned, and in particular the lumbar and sacral regions were much more active. Over 75 percent of this group were able to bend and touch their toes, while only 16 percent of the others managed it. Finally, cholesterol levels were lower in the Tai Chi group, though this can also apply to other forms of exercise.

With age people feel less inclined to take exercise, but the exercise of Tai Chi is gentle and slow. This means that little demand is made on the heart, and yet Tai Chi conducts the blood supply to and from the extremities of the body, indeed to all parts of the body, helping to prevent the buildup of waste products due to poor circulation.

Although I have no data on the mental state of older Tai Chi practitioners, it is likely that mobility of their joints and good blood supply promote a happier outlook and ample oxygen for the brain. If a person gradually loses the capacity to move, this is almost bound to affect his or her attitude to, and enjoyment of life.

Though not specifically a result of Tai Chi training, all the above benefits can promote the possibility of sexual activity into later life, since this depends primarily on good health.

60

FINDING A TEACHER

Now that Tai Chi is a worldwide subject, attracting more and more students looking for teachers every day, it is unfortunately necessary to start this section with a warning. Students mean money, and money can mean con artists. You may remember what happened in the 1970s when Bruce Lee and Kung fu rocketed into popularity. So how do you know that a teacher is the genuine article?

You cannot learn Tai Chi only from a book, although this can inspire you and help you to remember what you learned in the class. So after finding a teacher try to talk to his or her pupils. What are their impressions and experiences? Is the teacher always trying to sell them books, tapes, and equipment which they do not need? Is the teacher conceited and self-absorbed, always criticizing other teachers? This all happens and has to be taken into account.

Of course, teachers come in all psychological and physical shapes and sizes. One person may not know a great deal, but may still be a good teacher. Another may know a great deal but be a poor teacher. In brief, shop around before you part with your time and money. What people learn with their first teacher tends to stick and be hard to eradicate, if it needs to be.

Always keep your feet on the ground. Tai Chi begins and ends with the way you move and feel inside. No amount of philosophy and words can replace this. If you want to think about Tai Chi and discuss it, then you should find a Chinese philosophy seminar.

An extension of this piece of advice is that you should persevere. Learn at least one Form so that

A teacher should find time for personal attention. A teacher should SHOW you what he or she wants you to do.

you can do it without forgetting what comes next. This will give you a good grounding. You will be able to do something which has a beginning, a middle, and an end. However, you may come across a teacher who emphasizes correct physical movement before an entire Form is learned. This should not discourage you. It is a subject that you would have to tackle sooner or later anyway; it has just arrived sooner. If you have any doubts about your health – joints, vertebrae, heart, etc. – get a medical checkup first, or at least ask your doctor's opinion to be on the safe side. Any medical condition

should be reported to your teacher before the first lesson.

More than anything, after perseverance, you will need patience and appreciation – which are closely linked. Tai Chi appreciation depends on noticing and seeing the significance of things which you might ordinarily ignore or dismiss as not worthy of attention. For example, if you occasionally notice that during your class you take a *relaxed and naturally deeper breath* than usual, appreciate it. It will probably be some time before your breathing deepens when doing the whole Form, but this experience is a taste of things to come. Then you will need patience to work and wait for it.

Useful Addresses

Teachers below can help with questions. Always send a stamped addressed envelope.

Kumar Frantzis
1 Cascade Drive
Fairfax, CA 94930

Kenneth Cohen
PO Box 234
Nederland, CO 80466

Nan Lu
396 Broadway (5th floor)
New York, NY 10013

Peter Chema
60 McClean Avenue
Yonkers, NY 10705

Daniel Crawford
Peacable Hill
Brewster, NY 10509

Bonnie Newman
52870 E. Cherryhill Drive
Sandy, OR 97055

Rick Schmoyer
1907 Electric Street
Dunmore, PA 18512

Reading List

Yearning K. Chen, *Tai Chi Chuan* (Hong Kong, 1971).

Chang Chung-yuan, *Creativity & Taoism* (Wildwood House, 1973).

Paul Crompton, *Chinese Soft Exercise, A Tai Chi Workbook* (Allen & Unwin, 1986).

Paul Crompton, *Elements of Tai Chi* (Element Books, 1990).

Paul Crompton, *Tai Chi for Two* (published by authors, 1995).

Paul Crompton, *Tai Chi Workbook* (Shambhala Publications, 1987).

Tomio Hirai, *Zen and the Mind* (Japan Publications, 1978).

Ted J. Kaptchuk, *Chinese Medicine, The Web that has no Weaver* (Rider, 1983).

Cheng Man-ch'ing, Lao-tze – *"My words are very easy to understand"* (North Atlantic Books, 1981).

Cheng Man-ch'ing and Robert W. Smith, *Tai Chi* (Tuttle, 1967).

Lizelle Raymond, *To Live Within* (Allen & Unwin, 1972).

Paul Reps, *Zen Flesh, Zen Bones* (Penguin Books, 1957).

E. Dale Saunders, *Mudra* (Routledge 1960).

Bow Sim-Mark, *Simplified Tai Chi Chuan* (Boston, 1977).

Robert W. Smith, *Chinese Boxing, Masters and Methods* (Kodansha, 1973).

INDEX

Aknowledgments

Key: a=above b=below l=left r=right

Images Colour Library 1; Sipa Press/Rex Features 4, 5;
Flip Chalfant/Image Bank 6a; E.T. Archive 10;
G.A. Rossi/Image Bank 14br; R. Wahstrom/Image Bank 16br;
E.T. Archive 18br; Tom Owen Edmunds/Image Bank 46bl;
Pictor 47a; Bill Bachmann/Ace 47b; Grant V. Faint/ Image Bank 48a;
Pictor 52; Karl Ammann/Ace 53b Sipa Press/Rex Features 54b;
Mauritius/Ace 56; Nigel Hicks/Ace 58; Ronnie Robinson 59.

All other photographs are the copyright of Quarto Publishing plc.

Quarto would like to thank Emily Yeung Mei Ling
for the Chinese calligraphy on pages 4 and 45.